Passive Income

The Top 5 Ways to Make Money Online Becoming Financially FREE in 60 Days or Less!

Stop Working and Start Living Today!

Introduction

I want to thank you and congratulate you for purchasing the book, *"Passive Income: The Top 5 Ways to Make Money Online Becoming Financially FREE in 60 Days or Less! Stop Working and Start Living Today!"*.

This book contains proven steps and strategies on how to establish your own source of passive income, and have an additional stream of funds to help you achieve financial stability.

First things first: passive income doesn't mean no effort at all. Like a tree that bears fruit, you'll have to start with a seed to plant and cultivate. It's not free money – it's something that requires upfront work.

There are different ways on how you can establish a stream of passive income: some choose to create mobile apps, spend money on investments and real estate, sell items on garage sales and flea markets, and to get involved in web-related activities such as blogging and affiliate marketing – all are included in this book.

Having a source of passive income will help you not only to be productive during idle time, but also to make more money along the process. Passive income can lead to a better financial status, or better yet, financial stability. That's something you'd want, wouldn't you?

Thanks again for purchasing this book, I hope you enjoy it!

☐ **Copyright 2016 by Spirit Publishing- All rights reserved.**

This document is geared towards providing exact and reliable information in regards to the topic and issue covered. The publication is sold with the idea that the publisher is not required to render accounting, officially permitted, or otherwise, qualified services. If advice is necessary, legal or professional, a practiced individual in the profession should be ordered.

- From a Declaration of Principles which was accepted and approved equally by a Committee of the American Bar Association and a Committee of Publishers and Associations.

In no way is it legal to reproduce, duplicate, or transmit any part of this document in either electronic means or in printed format. Recording of this publication is strictly prohibited and any storage of this document is not allowed unless with written permission from the publisher. All rights reserved.

The information provided herein is stated to be truthful and consistent, in that any liability, in terms of inattention or otherwise, by any usage or abuse of any policies, processes, or directions contained within is the solitary and utter responsibility of the recipient reader. Under no circumstances will any legal responsibility or blame be held against the publisher for any reparation, damages, or monetary loss due to the information herein, either directly or indirectly.

Respective authors own all copyrights not held by the publisher.

The information herein is offered for informational purposes solely, and is universal as so. The presentation of the information is without contract or any type of guarantee assurance.

The trademarks that are used are without any consent, and the publication of the trademark is without permission or backing by the trademark owner. All trademarks and brands within this book are for clarifying purposes only and are the owned by the owners themselves, not affiliated with this document.

Table of Contents

Introduction i

Chapter 1 – What is Passive Income? 1

Passive Income # 1: Mobile App Creation 13

Passive Income # 2: Investments 24

Passive Income # 3: Real Estate 35

Passive Income # 4:Flea Markets, Garage Sales and other Sales-Related Activities... 46

Passive Income # 5: Web-Related Activities............... 55

Conclusion 69

Chapter 1 – What is Passive Income?

To obtain financial freedom, one must be either a business owner, an investor, or both, generating passive income, particularly on a monthly basis.

– Robert Kiyosaki

Imagine waking up each morning realizing that you no longer have to scramble and be stressed about paying the bills. Imagine checking out any payments due, and then feel relieved because you have enough to settle them all.

That's all possible – through your passive income.

Earning isn't limited to you getting up early and going to your 8-5 job five or six days a week – you can also earn as you sleep, eat, cook... whatever you want.

Again, that's all possible – through your passive income.

What is Passive Income?

Passive income is the flow of money coming to you that doesn't need as much maintenance or may not need maintenance at all. You don't have to be materially active to produce this income flow – you just have to get it going, and then it'll earn money on its own with little upkeep.

With passive income, you may need to invest lots of time, money and energy to get it started. When things go well, though, it's going to pay for itself and no time. This is when you can even say that you earn money while you sleep.

There are different ways on how you can earn passive income – a few of them are described in this book. How should you choose? Well, it all depends on what your interests are, and which one will you be willing to learn.

WHY IS PASSIVE INCOME IMPORTANT?

Two reasons: financial stability and time.

It's important to have a source of passive income; this is not to make you lazy but because it'll help you achieve that goal – ***financial stability***. Admit it, it's so hard to be stressed just because you'd have to pay the bills, and your salary will hardly make it.

Here's some good news: an extra $50 or $100 will go a long way. A much better news: that amount – $50-$100 – is highly achievable.You just need to exert a little bit of effort – okay, maybe a LOT of effort –and it will earn you that money sooner than you expect.

Time, on the other hand, is more tempting for some. Having a steady stream of passive income may allow you to reach your goals – perhaps for retirement, a special purchase or for other personal purposes – earlier, giving you more time to spend on whatever reason you want.

Whether you're after time or financial stability, it all boils down to one thing: you should have a source of passive income.

COMMON MISCONCEPTIONS ABOUT PASSIVE INCOME

There are common myths and misconceptions surrounding passive income. Before you proceed with various methods of earning passive income, it's best to get this all cleared first.

- *Earning passive income will quickly make you rich.* – These aren't get-rich-quick schemes. To earn passive income, you still have to invest a substantial amount of time, money, and/or energy. You won't make money out of doing nothing. It's not like winning the lottery; it won't make money overnight.

- *You can set it all up, and once it's earning money, then you can forget all about it.*–You still have to maintain it. It won't require as much effort compared to when you were still starting, but you still have to exert efforts to keep it. You would have to monitor it from time to time to see what you have to improve on, any maintenance projects or any possible enhancements.

- *Only rich people can find ways to earn passive income.* – Anyone can earn passive income. If you're struggling financially, the more you may want to consider checking out passive income. There are passive income sources that don't require much money such as blogging and holding garage sales; take advantage of these options instead.

- *"Now that I have passive income sources, I can now leave my job."* – Passive income should only be there to supplement your main income source; besides, your source of passive income doesn't always start as lucrative. You'll be lucky enough if your passive income source becomes so successful that it'll become your main income source, but it usually is just a back-up source of resource.

A lot of people have wrong impressions toward passive income; that's why it's best to clarify all doubts before you proceed.

BENEFITS OF PASSIVE INCOME

No matter what venture you're in, having a stream of passive income will always be a great help. Still unsure if you want to proceed? Get to know the perks of having this additional stream of money entering your accounts.

You'll earn for doing something that you love.

You've heard all about it: when you do what you love, then it'll feel like you'll never work a day in your life. It'll feel the same when you're earning for your passive income – you choose what to do and how you do it, so it won't feel as burdensome compared to how you'll feel if things were forced.

This is why more often than not, passive income sources are interests that have turned into lucrative hobbies, such as blogging and creating YouTube videos. You started doing it because it was something that you loved, and not because you immediately wanted money out of it. It just so happened that you found ways on how to get paid for it.

You'll enhance your talent.

Some passive income sources started out simply as a talent that found ways to earn money. As you progress, you find more ways to improve your talent, and you discover how you can earn more through these developments.

Your talent can still be enhanced even if you don't discover anything new (that rarely happens, though). What you can do is to keep on doing what you've been doing – you'll soon find yourself faster and better.

It allows you to save money.

When one establishes a source of passive income, he gets money that's separate from the main income source, and this leads to the production ofan additional stream of funds. These additional funds can be used in any matter that you prefer – whether to keep as an emergency fund, to save up for a special purchase or to reinvest in another passive income source.

Now that you have an idea on what passive income is and why it should be one of your priorities, then it's about time to choose which one you will go for as a source of passive income.

Passive Income # 1: Mobile App Creation

> *"Mobile is becoming not only the new digital hub, but also the bridge to the physical world. That's why mobile will affect more than just your digital operations — it will transform your entire business."*
>
> *- Thomas Husson*

Today, mobile phones are now considered not a luxury but a necessity. Is there anyone out there who doesn't own a smartphone? Kids and adults alike are aware of what apps are, and some are even willing to spend a few dollars for them.

Aside from its usual purposes such as making and receiving calls and SMS messages, mobile phones can also serve as music players, calculators, weight planners, schedulers, and so on and so forth.

App developers have this "need" in mind, hence it had led them to create mobile applications. It's actually a win-win situation, you see: the consumers buy their apps to help them with their needs, and you earn money as payment.

CREATING APPS AS A PASSIVE INCOME SOURCE

It's more ideal to create mobile apps compared to full scale software because it doesn't require as much programming, plus it can be tested sooner. If you're not too familiar with creating mobile apps, then you can ask the help of more experienced programmers to create the app for you.

There are various ways on how you can earn from mobile applications. You can create a free application and earn from paid ads and/or in-app purchases, create a paid application and earn from app payments and/or in-app purchases, or variations of the sort.

Ask the mobile creators of Snapchat, Flappy Bird, Candy Crush and Angry Birds; they're sure to tell you that the right app can make you earn money.

HOW APP CREATIONS CAN LEAD TO PASSIVE INCOME

How will your app lead to passive income? There are several ways.

One, you can make a *freemium* app or game. Freemium games or apps are those that are offered free at first, but with limited features or content. If users need those content, then they can pay for it through in-app purchases.

You can offer the game for free and let users enjoy the game, and once they're hooked, then it'll be easy for them to purchase and pay for the app.

Two, you can create *an app that you have to pay for one time.* Once the app is paid for, then you can access everything. Any feature additions and updates are free of charge.

When launching a paid app, you have to remember to make it so awesome that users will not hesitate to pay for it, even if they haven't tried it out yet.

Three, you can create a *free app but with advertising.* You can download the app for free, but you'll have to view advertisements as you use it. You earn more if there are a lot of people who have downloaded the app, and if they are using the app frequently.

Your mobile app can easily turn into a passive income source as long as it has been used and downloaded, so make one that'll easily get people's attention and make them hooked.

MOBILE APP INSPIRATIONS

Still hesitant? Here's a bit of inspiration to get you started.

Candy Crush Saga

King had encountered a lot of issues before it got to creating *Candy Crush Saga* – its creators even experienced not getting any salary for the first year. It first focused on creating web-based games before switching to mobile applications. Candy Crush Saga wasn't even its first mobile app but it turned out the most successful – not only it earned hundreds of millions as early as 2011, but it also led King to launch an initial public offering (IPO).

Flappy Bird

Flappy Bird was a surprise hit, even for its creator Dong Nguyen. Nguyen created a number of apps prior to Flappy Bird, but nothing came close to the popularity of Flappy Bird.

Flappy Bird was all about a chunky bird that you have to maneuver by tapping the screen. No complications – all you had to do was to avoid the obstacles and to earn points by flying past the pipes. That's all it was. But it took the world by storm because it was too addicting.Nguyen was then receiving around $50,000 from the ads on the game.

Nguyen wasn't able to endure the difficulties that came with the game, and so, he ended up taking the game down. Still, he's a proof that with the right game, you can achieve a lot – perhaps a lot more than you've hoped for.

Snapchat

Snapchat was launched in 2011, and is now one of the most popular social networking apps for mobile users. Its most popular feature is its "disappearing message" feature, and this feature made Snapchat unique among other social media sites.

Snapchat is a free application, and you don't see ads displayed on it. So how does it earn money? It earns money when it receives money from bigger companies such as Alibaba and Yahoo! for additional funding, and through its feature called "Discover" which allows publishers to have their content featured on Snapchat.

WHAT YOU NEED TO REMEMBER

If you think users will be downloading your app but won't be using them as much, then on your end it'll be better to charge $0.99 for it – you'll end up having higher revenue than you expected.

On the other hand, if the app you're creating will have high user engagement, then it'll be better to go for an ad-supported application. You'll make money in this manner; just make sure you won't have any problems with the ad networks.

There are apps that don't work well with ads, so what you do is to give it for free, but implement in-app purchases. For example, users can pay for power-ups, additional lives, more energy, and related items. With this, users can enjoy the game while not being bothered by ads, but you still earn at the process.

If you choose to launch paid apps, you have to remember that it's hard to have repeat revenue, so you have to be on the lookout for new customers. Some mobile app developers create paid apps with additional features to pay for, but you have to be careful in making these, because not everyone will be happy with this.

With the amount of time spent by people in their mobile phones today, it won't be a bad idea to invest on mobile apps to achieve a steady stream of passive income. All you need is a good idea for an app and make it happen.

Passive Income # 2: Investments

"Someone's sitting in the shade today because someone planted a tree a long time ago."

– *Warren Buffett*

Warren Buffett's right, isn't he? He definitely has a good idea on how investments work as a passive income source. Someone planted a tree years ago, watered it, took care of it, let the sun shine on it... and now he – or someone else – will benefit from the shade it gives.

That's why investments are ideal sources of passive income.

Investments don't only work as a means to save for retirement, or a way to gather funds for a particular period of time – it can also help you have money for your short-term needs.

Those who use investments as a source of passive income – also known as 'passive traders' –are those who don't have a lot of time to spend to monitor their investments.If you're too busy because of a full-time job or because of another income source, then this is ideal for you.

WHY CHOOSE INVESTMENTS?

It's a good idea to have investments as a source of passive income.

Stocks, for example, have a tendency of having unlimited gains; there's no limit on how high they could go. The stock you bought today for $10 could go as high as $100 tomorrow with the right triggers. And so, you can have higher capital gains.

Dividends, on the other hand, are ideal sources as well of passive income. Companies often issue dividends on a regular basis (unless they decide to stop it), so if you've invested on stocks that issue dividends, then you can be assured that you'll receive them on a specific time.

With options, you can set it up in a way that you'll receive the premium regardless if the stock price goes up or down. Either way, you'll be receiving money – again, in the form of the premium.

If you do this well, then you can expect a lot of profit even if you don't spend your time monitoring your stock every now and then. Unlike active traders, you don't have to be bothered by little changes happening in the market and you don't choose to be contented with short-term gains.

IDEAL INVESTMENTS FOR PASSIVE INCOME STREAM

There are different kinds of investments that can lead to passive income. Some of them involve owning stocks and investing on options. Get to know these investments – see which ones will be fit for you and ideal for your lifestyle.

Investing in Stocks with Dividends

There are stocks that not only show possibilities of growth, but also give you a share of their earnings especially if the company has performed well.

There are two kinds of dividends: cash and stock dividends.*Cash dividends* are given in the form of cash, and of course *stock dividends* are in the form of stocks, added to your portfolio.

With dividend stocks, you have two ways to earn.

- One, you can collect the dividend itself once it's added to your portfolio. You can withdraw the dividends and use it in whatever manner you may wish.

- Two, you can reinvest the dividends and buy more stocks. In this manner, you'll end up with more shares, and that means more dividends when the company gives them again.

Cash dividends work both ways as well – you either take them out or use them to buy more stocks. Either way, you get to benefit from the dividends issued to you.

Dividends are ideal sources of passive income especially if you've invested in companies that grow in rates that are higher than inflation. Dividends have high potential for growth, even with the volatility of the market. As long as your dividend-earning stocks are there in your portfolio, then you may receive your dividend.

You just don't go claiming dividends, though. There is a specific rule in receiving dividends:

A company announces that they'll be issuing dividends on a particular date i.e. the *declared date*. You'll have to own the stock on or before the *ex-dividend date* (usually two business days after the declared date) to be entitled to the dividend. Then, a list will be released on the *record date* – if you owned the stock on the ex-dividend date, then your name will be included in the list.

Hence, be aware of the dates when companies give dividends – this actually determines if you'll be getting those dividends or not.

Owning and Selling Stocks

With owning and selling stocks, you have chances of getting *capital gains*. Capital gains is the profit you receive when you sell stocks in a price higher than the price you've bought them for. (Capital loss is when you sell it in a lower price.)

You're likely going to have capital gains if the stock price goes up. Rising stock prices don't always lead to capital gains if you have bought them in prices higher than the average, so it has to rise much higher for you to claim capital gains. When selling stocks, it's not just the price – you also have to consider the fees to be charged along the way.

If you wanted capital gains in just a short time, then it'll be possible with a little help from your friend, *technical analysis.* Technical analysis allows you to predict how the stock price will go through the use of charts – it'll tell you if the price will increase, decrease or stay where it is. Hence, choose promising stocks that indicate possible rising prices through its charts, and steer clear of those that show decline of prices.

Options Trading

Some choose to get involved in options trading, and they earn passive income along the way. In options trading, you earn income through buying premiums – buying premiums mean that you'll be receiving them regardless of the direction of the market.

Your passive income usually comes from "writing" or selling stock options, or selling calls and puts. (Selling calls means selling stocks and selling puts means buying stocks.) When you write stock options, the premium is yours regardless if the stock price goes higher or lower.

Some choose to go for covered calls i.e. *long call + long stock* because they can be approved for IRAs – this means you can add them up to your retirement accounts. However, covered calls (and options trading itself) can be quite tricky and confusing especially for beginners so it's not preferred by most.

Passive Income # 3: Real Estate

"There have been few things in my life which have had a more genial effect on my mind than the possession of a piece of land"

— Harriet Martineau

You've probably learned that land is the only asset that doesn't depreciate; in fact, its value appreciates as time progresses. You can take advantage of that reality by using it as a stream of passive income through real estate.

Let's face it – real estate seems to be the hardest to establish with regard to passive income, simply because it may require a higher amount of investment to get it going.

With real estate, there's a lot of risk involved, and you can't be assured of profits anytime soon.

There are people who have succeeded, so that means you could succeed in making real estate a source of passive income too. It's a common way for people to achieve wealth, so why shouldn't you try it out yourself?

WHY REAL ESTATE?

Why should you choose real estate as a passive income source?

One, because **you get to be the bossof your venture**. You get to choose everything:

from the type of property you'd be investing in, how much you'll charge for fees i.e. rent etc. and who will be utilizing your property.

Two, **the money you earn goes straight to your pocket**. This is most applicable to rental properties after all fees have been settled – their rent payments go straight to your bank accounts, unless you're going to use a portion or the full amount for fees and/or maintenance.There are landlords who can't pocket every amount yet because of repairs and mortgage payments, but once everything is all covered, then it's all yours.

Three, **there are no limits to where you can go**. You can gain a lot of leverage when you invest in real estate, and so you have a lot of opportunities available and have higher chances of increasing your overall return on investment.

Four, **there are tax advantages involved**. Investing in real estate is a good way to cut your taxes. Through depreciation, you can recover costs of income-producing properties. There's also what you call the 1031 Exchange – you can defer your taxes through the sale of an investment property and then using to purchase another one with equal or higher value within a particular amount of time.

Five, **you can get possible tax write-offs against other income**. Of course, it's best to check this first with tax professionals, but there are chances of you receiving tax deductions that can be used against other sources of income.

Six, your **cash flow can be tax-free**. Another advantage of investing in real estate is that your cash flow can be tax-free because of deductions from mortgage interests and depreciation.

You've read six, but there are definitely a lot more reasons why you should invest in real estate and make it a source of passive income. If you have the resources, then don't hesitate to invest in real estate – it'll be worth every penny you spend. Every man needs a roof under his head, so you'll always have a potential customer when you invest in real estate.

REAL ESTATE RELATED INVESTMENTS

There are different forms of investments related to real estate that can become a source of passive income.

Take your pick among the following:

Rental Properties

The process of owning land and having them rented have been practiced years ago. It's an ideal passive income source because you don't have to do a lot of work to keep it – as long as you check the area every now and then, then you're good to go.

You own the land and have it rented, so you become the landlord who is in charge of paying for taxes, mortgage and maintenance costs. Lacking finances? Filing for a loan or asking the help from a trusted partner will be ideal to implement. Again, the rental income can cover them later on, as long as the rightful maintenance is performed.

To cover all those aforementioned costs, the landlord will charge rent – not too excessive but just reasonable enough to make profit – and will entirely become passive income once all costs have been settled and paid for.

Challenges with rental properties include having bad tenants or damages to the property – in these cases you'd have to shoulder the costs first and then make up for it later on. As long as you have the right property, then finding tenants for it won't be a problem; you'll just have to screen them to find the suitable ones.

Real Estate Investment Trusts (REITs)

Real Estate Investment Trusts or REITs are also a good form of investment that can lead to a steady stream of passive income. REITs allow you to invest in real estate without having to own or buy individual properties. It's created when a trust or corporation uses investors' funds to purchase and manage income properties.

REITs have to share 90% of the taxable profits to its investors in dividend form so it can keep its REIT status; in turn, it won't have to pay corporate income taxes. Investors will receive regular income because of the dividends it regularly issues, plus investments are highly liquid – you can easily cash them out when needed.

Real Estate Trading (Flipping)

There are people who buy properties to have them rented. There are land owners on the other hand who choose to buy properties with the intent of selling them later on.

Real estate traders will only hold their property in a short-term basis and will aim to sell them for profits. Traders go for those undervalued properties or those that are in very hot markets. Some flippers choose to not invest any additional money on the property – this becomes a short-term investment for them.

Land Ownership

Owning a piece of land isn't so bad, especially that the value of land gets higher as time passes. You can consult with a tax professional on how you can take advantage of depreciation, but it's one way on why land ownership is a good source of passive income.

It may be considered passive income because you'll be able to get something out of it if you choose to sell it, have it rented, or utilize it for an income-producing venture.

BOTTOM LINE

Perhaps you've seen by now why investing in real estate is ideal for those who want a stream of passive income. Take your pick among those mentioned – which one appeals most to you? Rental properties? REITs? Whatever your choice is, it's bound to be a good source of passive income.

Passive Income # 4: Flea Markets, Garage Sales and other Sales-Related Activities

"To make money you have to use a four letter word: SELL."

– Richie Norton

Got things at home that you no longer use? Got items that only collect dust on their shelves? Know how to create things? You can use them to earn as well.

FLEA MARKETS / GARAGE SALES

Do you have anything at home that you no longer use? Any stuff at home that you'd wish to discard but are still useful? You can earn from them by selling them on flea markets, or by setting up your own garage sale.

For all you know, someone'll love to have the stuff you're thinking of throwing out, so you might as well sell them so you can earn additional income.

Garage Sale Flipping

There are those people who have seen garage sales in a different light; what they do is to visit garage sales and buy items that they can possibly sell for a higher amount.

Be alert; who knows, you might see these items in garage sales:

a. *New and/or Sealed Items*–Any item that is new and sealed – more so if in its original packaging –will have twice (or even thrice) of its value. You can even sell vintage items as new, as long as they are sealed.

b. *Used Clothing* –There are people who sell used clothes in garage sales – even branded clothing items. Some of these clothes can be so cheap that you can buy them for $1. These used clothes you can resell in sites for decent prices.

c. *Vintage Collectibles* – If you like checking out garage sales, then you also have to do your research – particularly about vintage collectibles. It's not impossible to see collectible items in garage sales, and learn to identify which ones are actually worth a lot of money. Collectors have a variety of niches to choose from; you just have to know where to look and what to look for.

d. *Used Books*–There are people who sell used books with the thought of purchasing newer ones – these are moments you can take advantage of. Books have potential for earning huge profits, especially upon finding rare and/or signed books.Storing books isn't a problem, and shipping them isn't difficult either.

Garage sale flipping is a good idea, don't you think? Get out there and check out garage sales – who knows what you'll find?

AFFILIATE MARKETING

Affiliate marketing is also another popular way to earn passive income. This method is one of those passive income ways wherein you don't have to shell out money, but instead spend lots of time and energy.

Affiliate marketing is ideal for blogs especially those that are attracting high amounts of traffic. The more people that visit the site, the higher chances of having people click on your site's links, making you earn money.

The amount you get from affiliate marketing is truly passive; to earn, you don't have to do anything – all people do is to click on your ads, and nothing else.

How to Earn through Affiliate Marketing

With affiliate marketing, all you need is to use your website or blogsite. You'll be given codes and instructions on how to 'embed' or how to place the advertisements on your blog.

Now that you have your site up and running, you can then arrange for your site to advertise products. All you need is for someone to click the link for the product advertised; if the visitor ends up buying, then you'll get a commission from the sales.

The tip here is to choose products that fit well with whatever you're discussing. Why? It's because the people who visit your site are often there for the content, and your products should match what you're offering.

Examples of Affiliate Marketing Sites

- Amazon Affiliate Program – Amazon's affiliate program seems little, but Amazon's wide range of products make it attractive for affiliates. You'll find it easy to use and navigate the site regardless if you're a beginner or a pro.Some may find the starting rate for commissions smaller than the usual, but can be acceptable if it's not your main income source.

- ClickBank–ClickBank is ideal for those who are vendors of digital products and gadgets. You'd love its history of timely payments and its wide variety of electronic items. Compared to other markets, commission rates are also higher; for every sale, you can get around 50-75 percent.

- Google AdSense – Run by Google, this affiliate program gives publishers a unique ID to use for their accounts. This unique ID will be able to produce ad codes that can be used to earn cash.

With AdSense, there are various ways on how you can earn; you're not limited to posting ads on your site.

Amazon Affiliate Program, ClickBank and Google AdSense are just three of the most popular affiliate programs that you can take advantage of; if these three don't meet your standards, then don't worry – there are lots out there that you can choose from.

Once you've set everything up, then all you need is wait – soon you'll receive your first dollar... and it'll take it from there.

Passive Income # 5: Web-Related Activities

"Create a link through which you can market your dream products. Create a blog or a website of your own depending on what you want to be recognized for. Share your experiences through these media."

— Israelmore Ayivor

The Internet has made a lot of things possible; among these things is a possibility of earning passive income. If you're one of those who spend their time just sitting in front of their computer, letting their hours go by, then you might want to try this out.

Web-related activities such as blogging and creating YouTube videos are some of your hobbies that you can turn into a lucrative venture. These seem like ordinary activities that you just do for fun, but why not turn them into something that you can earn from, right?

BLOGGING

Blogging has become popular for both young and old people. A blog, a shortened form of the phrase *'web log'*, is a website that's regularly updated. It can be run either by an individual or a group of people; topics usually are discussed in an informal manner.

Blogging has become an online journal for some – a place where they share where they've been, what they've eaten, who they met, etc. It's a way to share their thoughts and to find people with similar interests.

Blogging as a Passive Income Source

There are two ways on how you can use your blog as a passive income source: one, the blog itself will earn, or two, the blog will help launch the actual passive income source.

The blog will be an effective seller if it meets three things: good content, post context and commerce.

- Content – Your readers will keep coming back as long as they see educational, useful and entertaining content. They should read information based on the product and whether it satisfies your readers' needs and wants.

- Context – Sure, your main aim is to make sales, but you also have to consider your blog posts' context. Provide details such as information about the product, how it should be used and why consumers should buy it.

- Commerce – Now that you've supplied all details necessary and hopefully answered all questions inside your readers' minds, then it might be time for them to finally purchase the item by using their credit cards. Guide consumers on how to buy the item in your site to make things easier for them.

As long as your content and products meet the clients' needs, then it'll be easy to sell through your blog.

Earnings from Blogs

Your blog itself can serve as your passive income source; just make sure you've got great content on it. Having good and relevant content, as well as applying SEO techniques will bring your blog page to the first page of search engine results, bringing more traffic.

There are bloggers who also earn through their product reviews. Some choose to review items such as electronic items and gadgets, and then post their 'findings' on their blog.

Product reviews are particularly helpful to those who are still 'shopping around' – your review may determine whether they'll buy the product or not.

Blogs as a Selling Platform

What items can be sold through your blogs? A lot of items, such as:

- Clothing – Clothing items are also popular in being sold in blogs. You can place their pictures for people to choose from.

- Craft items – Have hobbies? Like collecting stuff? You can sell them in your blog; display them through posting pictures and details about every item.

Being familiar with shipping and payment options will also be beneficial.

- Books and/ or E-books – E-books are becoming more popular nowadays because of its portability. Promote reading by selling e-books and books in your site.

- Online courses – If you're good at something and you can teach as well, then you might as well teach online courses. The online platform is ideal as it can reach a lot of people, so a lot of people can benefit from the courses you sell.

...and a lot more. There's no limit to what you can sell in your blog.

YOUTUBE VIDEO CREATION

Would you want to earn back the money you spent in making videos? Are you thinking of making them as a form of passive income? YouTube can make it possible.

Having an account allows you to not only watch videos, create playlists and the like. You can also set it up in a way that it'll become a source of passive income.

Interested? Read on.

Setting Up Your YouTube Account

First, you have to create your YouTube account. One of the easiest methods is to use your Google account, and then you're good to go.

(Some, on the other hand, choose to create their own accounts right then and there – that'll also work just fine.)

Next, have your channel enabled for monetization. Have the channel connected to a Google AdSense account – this'll allow you to earn from your monetized videos.

Here are the minimum requirements for a video to be monetized:

- The content has to be advertiser-friendly.

- You're responsible for creating the content, or you've been given permission for its commercial use.

- You have proof and documentation that both audio and video content are all yours.

- The content abides with both YouTube's Community Guidelines and Terms of Service. Not being compliant may prevent your account from being monetized.

As long as your videos follow these guidelines, then you have great chances of YouTube approving your videos for monetization.There are videos that require additional requirements – you'll be informed in these cases.

Once your account is approved by YouTube, then you can already earn from it by placing advertisements and through earning opportunities.

Other Ways to Earn

Aside from earning through your videos, there are also ways on how you can take advantage of YouTube to establish your passive income stream, such as:

- *Collaboration with brands.* Ad agencies and brands are always finding ways to promote their products; your channel can be a good way for them to reach out to other audiences, especially if your audience meets their target market.

- *Fan funding.* There are areas where YouTube is allowing content creators to place a tip-in jar on their channel so their audience can provide monetary support. Not all regions allow this, though, so check first to see if you can have this happen on your account.

- *Merchandising.* To spread your popularity, you can create merchandise for your brand, or receive items from sponsors to give away to your viewers. You can also ask them to spread the word and to promote your channel so you can broaden your reach.

As you can see, this will be more effective if you've already established a following for a site. But of course, you can also take advantage of these methods regardless if you're a newcomer as long as you know how to do it well.

To add, like what was mentioned earlier, not every region allows these ideas – check first with your area if you can have your idea take place.

Conclusion

Thank you again for purchasing this book!

I hope this book was able to help you to understand what passive income is, its importance, and which activities can help you gain a stream of passive income.

The next step is to choose among the various activities enumerated in the previous chapters. You have a lot to choose from – it's all up to you which one you'll go for.

Which attracts you the most? Creating apps, blogs and videos? Real estate? Selling stuff you no longer need? Investing on dividend-earning stocks? It's all up to you, depending on what your interests are, how much time you can spend, and how much money you're willing to spend – so you can earn.

You don't have to settle on a single source of passive account; for example, you can maintain a blog while holding a garage sale. You're not limited to one source; as long as you can manage them properly, then it's all up to you.

Remember that when your income exceeds your expenses, then you may have finally achieved what other people are simply dreaming of: financial stability. So don't be scared to take the risk – you'll never know until you try.

Finally, if you enjoyed this book, then I'd like to ask you for a favor, would you be kind enough to leave a review for this book on Amazon? It'd be greatly appreciated!

Thank you and good luck!

www.ingramcontent.com/pod-product-compliance
Lightning Source LLC
Chambersburg PA
CBHW070133210526
45170CB00013B/863